Wallace Milroy's
MALT WHISKY
ALMANAC

A TASTER'S GUIDE

ST. MARTIN'S PRESS•NEW YORK

ISBN 0-312-06542-6

Wallace Milroy's Malt Whisky Almanac.
Copyright © 1991 by Lochar Publishing Ltd.

Library of Congress Cataloging in Publication Data

(available on request)

Edited by Neil Wilson
Designed by Roger Hammond, London
Drawings on pages 22, 87
by William McClymont
Maps by David Langworth
Typesetting by Chapterhouse of Formby L37 3PX
Printed in Scotland by Eagle Colour Books Ltd

Lochar Publishing and St. Martin's Press gratefully
acknowledges the assistance of the Keepers of The Quaich
in the production of this work.

First published in Great Britain by Lochar Publishing.
First U.S. Edition: September 1991

10 9 8 7 6 5 4 3 2 1

CONTENTS

ACKNOWLEDGEMENTS

For over five years I have given due thanks here to everyone who has been associated with the production of this book. However I feel the time has come to simply thank everyone in the whisky industry for their unceasing help and hospitality in the annual revision and update of material for each edition. The past four years has seen the establishment of some new facilities designed to aid in the education of anyone seeking a knowledge of Scotch and to this end I have listed below the most prominent contacts in the field who are always willing and ready to help anyone with a thirst for malt whisky.

USEFUL ADDRESSES

The Scotch Malt Whisky Association
17 Half Moon Street
LONDON W1
Tel: 071–629–4384
Permanent displays on the workings of a distillery with models and Audio-Visual. Admission free.

The Scotch Malt Whisky Society
87 Giles Street
LEITH EH6 6BZ
Tel: 031–554–3451
Offering 10 to 20 cask strength malts, usually around 60% and up to 21 years old. Introductory membership fee is £30 including a bottle of malt.

The Scotch Whisky Heritage Centre
358 Castlehill
The Royal Mile
EDINBURGH
EH1 2NE
Tel: 031–220–0441
Admission from £1.25. Audio-visual, guided tours, retail outlet.

The Malt Whisky Association
LARGS
Ayrshire
KA30 8BR
Tel: 0475–676376
Membership: £12.50 p.a. Magazine, special offers, mail order whiskies.

FOREWORD

F
ew thought that the Society of Keepers of the Quaich would, so swiftly, have drawn so many members from around the world into such agreeable company. Yet, this is the case and as a useful reminder of the contemplative beauty of both Scotland and her whisky, this Almanac written by the world's leading connoisseur, Wallace Milroy, must prove again its admirable value.

The Society is happy to be associated with this further edition, because we believe it will help to stimulate discussion and place the contrasting pleasures of the different whiskies in the most amiable light. May each whisky cheer your conversation and bring you a host of friends.

Broomhall, Fife
January 1991

Lord Elgin
Grand Master
Keeper of the Quaich

INTRODUCTION

Five years after publication of the first edition of this modest pocket guide, I am delighted once more to report that its success runs in parallel with the worldwide demand for single bottled malts. Sales are now 150,000 plus, still rising and the book is now available in Japanese, Italian and German language editions.

It is immensely rewarding for me to see the results of over a quarter of a century's association with bottled malts come to fruition in such a way and that my generic and simple tasting notes cross the language barriers comfortably. And so it should be. Scotch is a medium which should not need translating, and the generous variety of styles amongst Scotland's malts should provide plenty of banter amongst tasters from Tokyo to Tobermory! Long may it remain so.

In the past 18 months, the Japanese have at last revised their tax structure on spirits, thus allowing Scotch a somewhat more popular (or rather populous!) presence in the country. It is, however, still expensive by our standards. But it is a start at least, and one on which our exports can build more effectively.

Throughout 1990 the United States has continued and strengthened its love affair with malt as has Italy and France — and the German language edition speaks volumes for that country's growing interest in the cratur.

The international interest in malt continues at home and has not only manifested itself in enormous sales of bottled malts at the duty-free outlets and in areas where many foreign tourists are to be found, but also in the industry itself. Suntory have purchased a large share in one of our most popular whisky producers — Morrison Bowmore Distillers, who own Auchentoshan, Glen Garioch and Bowmore. Their influence will doubtless afford them access to quality fillings and allow them to establish a firm foothold in the hometrade industry. Nikka's ownership of Ben Nevis distillery is perhaps more apparent since one of the prime movers in their business had a Japanese father and a Scots mother and has as profound a knowledge of the product as anyone else in the business. Deanston distillery has for a long time been the subject of interest — much of it rumoured to be from France, however as I write I learn that a Glasgow firm Burn Stewart Distillers plc has secured the plant for the future at a cost of £2.1m. Allied Distillers have enlarged their malt portfolio to such an extent that Islay neighbours

Laphroaig and Ardbeg now find themselves in the same stable. The good news is that although they are both now indirectly under Canadian ownership, Ardbeg is now closer to being reopened than at any time since its sad closure in the early 80's, which I lamented in the last edition.

The UK producers have not been sleeping though and as we go to press, a number have undertaken the most simple (but very important) step of changing labels and/or bottle shape. Unfortunately, many will be coming onto the market after this book is produced so they may not be up to date at this moment. Don't despair, the content of the bottle is what really counts. Speaking of bottles, I heartily approve of those producers now making their malts available in half-bottles. This at least gives the taster the chance of trying two malts for the price of one — a useful tip for the tourist.

Some companies have been taking more fundamental steps. Highland Distilleries decided to deal with their comparatively poor export performance in a characteristically forthright manner. In the Autumn of 1990, Highland's chairman John Goodwin announced a cross-shareholding plan with Orpar, the controlling shareholder in Remy-Cointreau. Essentially Highland sold its 12.7% stake in Macallan-Glenlivet, purchased Orpar's Glenturret distillery and 25% of Orpar which may then buy a 10% stake in Highland in the future. This is the price Highland have paid for the power of Remy's distribution within some 20 overseas markets which should help transform Highland's export performance.

Essentially, the simple layout and format of this edition is the same as the last, although you may experience some difficulty in finding a few of the independently bottled malts whose availability is often dependent on the odd cache of butts lying at the rear of a quiet bond. If you find a bottle of St Magdalene, buy it, since the distillery has been converted into flats. We can, however, look forward in the not too distant future to an entirely new malt whisky — Kininvie from Dufftown. Wm Grant & Sons Ltd, owners of Glenfiddich and The Balvenie and for so long the innovators in the single bottled malt market, have not only decided that their fillings requirement justifies this increase in capacity, but also that their substantial expertise can be put to good use in the years to come in marketing a third malt.

This statement of faith in the future of malt can only be good. I personally have no doubt that malt whisky will continue to make friends throughout the world. When I

THE MALT WHISKY PRODUCING REGIONS OF SCOTLAND AND NORTHERN IRELAND.

pen the introduction to the next edition of this book I shall not be surprised to relate more good news regarding the industry.

For the moment though, we can indulge ourselves in what this book is about — tasting malt whisky, the pleasures that brings and why they differ so much. Why are there so many varieties? The differences can be detected broadly by sampling Bladnoch (from Galloway), Highland Park (from Orkney), Macallan (from Speyside) and Lagavulin (from Islay). Try them in a blind tasting and the chances are that even a beginner would detect the most obvious differences. These are attributable to each locality's distilling heritage — Lagavulin is pungent and smokey, illustrating the distillery's use of a peaty, soft source of water and Islay's tradition of using peat as a fuel when drying barley. The full bodied Macallan is silky-smooth as befits a whisky matured solely in sherry casks. Bladnoch — our most southerly malt whisky distillery — is distilled on a coast caressed by the Gulf Stream where delicate, tropical plants abound. It is light, estery and fragrant — the perfect pre-dinner dram whereas at our most northerly distillery at Highland Park, the malt has a smokey flavour imbued in it from the heather-covered Orkney peat moss which is burnt in the kilns. These characteristics show that whiskies are the living embodiment of their localities and the people who make them. As Jim McEwan, Manager of Bowmore Distillery has so often said, "The most important ingredient in malt whisky is the people who make it." Your preference for each malt will depend on the circumstances in which you drink it.

Within each producing region there are degrees of variation in taste, bouquet and colour which help create the hundred-plus bottled malts which are available in the UK. The alphabetical listing by region helps create not only a greater understanding of these regional variations but also of those subtle (and sometimes not so subtle) variances between malts within each region. This will all, I hope, allow you to appreciate the great depth of distilling tradition within Scotland and make your trip through the drams all the more enjoyable.

We begin on Speyside, where the greatest concentration of distilling activity in the world exists — over 50 distilleries in all. Then remaining in the Highlands we shall look at the Northern distilleries situated around Inverness and above the Moray Firth. To the East lie the distilleries nearer Banff, Aberdeen and the North Sea coast and in the

Southern region of the Highlands the activity is based
largely in rural Perthshire. Finally, moving over to the
Western part of the Highlands, three distilleries exist in
Fort William and Oban.

The Lowland region was once as busy as any other in
the making of whisky, but sadly that tradition has been
diminished in the last century. However, below the
imaginary line between Dundee and Greenock some nine
malts are available across the whole area.

Islay produces some of the most precious and
characterful malts and the product of all eight distilleries
on this beautiful island are available readily either as
brands or from the independent bottlers (see pages
138–139). Nearby Campbeltown, in Kintyre — once the
greatest whisky town of them all — now musters only three
malts. . . but they are wonderful drams nonetheless.

And finally the Island malts encompass the whiskies
of Jura, Mull (I am delighted to report that Tobermory
Distillery is now producing again, safe in the hands of Joe
Hughes who preceded Jim McEwan at Bowmore), Skye
and Orkney — each one differing from the other just as the
topography of their islands differs. You will again note the
inclusion of Bushmills malt from Northern Ireland. As I
stated in the last edition, the reason is simple enough. The
whiskey they produce may be in the Irish tradition, but it is
a true malt nevertheless and is produced within the
confines of the United Kingdom. To ignore it would be to
ignore an important contribution to this country's malt
whisky heritage.

All this helps to indicate where a whisky comes from
and what it tastes like, but I have never been inclined to use
the pages of this book as a means of telling the reader how
it is made. I have always assumed some foreknowledge of
the process but since so many real novitiates, confronted
by so much exposure and advertising, are asking how malt
is made — and rather than take up space here — I have
indicated in the introductory sections to each region and
on page 4 where to visit in order to understand the process
better. There are now some excellent establishments to
further one's knowledge but there is simply no substitute
for visiting a working distillery and being shown round by
the very people who make and are proud of their own
dram. Remember what Jim McEwan said ". . . the most
important ingredient".

SPEYSIDE

For many whisky enthusiasts malt whisky is most closely associated with Speyside, but in truth this is only half the story. The strength of the association, however, can be seen from the many distilleries which, although not situated beside the River Spey, make allegiance with it when stating their provenance.

The River Livet has also suffered from the same back-handed compliment and over the years many distillers (even true Speyside producers) claimed to produce "a Glenlivet", when strictly speaking they were stretching not only the geographical boundaries a bit far, but also the patience of the owners of the The Glenlivet Distillery itself. It all goes to show how over the last two centuries "Speyside" has meant high quality, and today the truth of that statement has not diminished at all.

The trade, however, has always tended to look at the large number of distilleries situated in this area as simply "Speysides", and for simplicity's sake I have continued with this categorisation for the Almanac. As you will see from the map over the page, the "Golden Triangle" really exists, stretching from Elgin over towards Banff and down to the cradle of distilling on Speyside — Dufftown. In this triangle lies the greatest concentration of malt whisky-making apparatus in the world, and to savour the atmosphere here is to realise how important and how dearly distilling is held in the Highlands of Scotland. Follow the "Whisky Trail" which is clearly signposted in this area and you will see what I mean.

The success of the Speyside distillers and their current profusion is due to the production of illicit whisky. At the end of the 18th Century, the Highland product was in such demand that the "protected" Lowland markets were infiltrated with the higher quality, smuggled produce of the illicit still. Finally, in 1823, an Act of Parliament betrayed

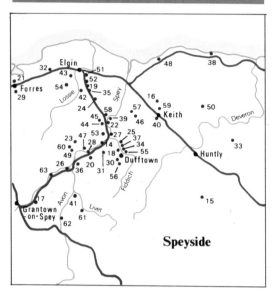

Speyside

Distillery location numbers refer to page numbers.

the fact that the Government had at last realised the best way to reduce the illicit trade was to make it attractive for the distillers to go legal. The Speyside men were, however, suspicious and only after George Smith, who distilled in Glenlivet, went legal in 1824 did they begin to accept the new laws.

Smith's foresight is manifested in the industry on Speyside as it stands today. Famous names abound — Macallan, Cardhu, Linkwood, Glenfiddich, Mortlach, Tamdhu — each and every one another experience to savour. Most of these distilleries can now cater for visitors in a number of ways and many of them have outstanding facilities which will not only make a visit to a typical Speyside distillery something to remember, but should also give a comprehensive (and comprehensible!) introduction to the processes involved in the production of fine malt whisky. Local Tourist

Information Centres will be able to give details of their local distilleries with these facilities, but where possible, I have indicated if a distillery can accommodate visitors, and how they can be contacted. Some of the more quick-witted producers like William Grant of Glenfiddich started catering for the visitor some time ago and can offer a day to remember. More recently United Distillers have developed visitor centres of particular appeal at Royal Lochnagar on Deeside, Blair Athol at Pitlochry and Cardhu near Knockando. Wherever you find yourself, be sure to try and visit one of them and buy a bottle of their malt.

Brand	**ABERLOUR**
Distillery	Aberlour ABERLOUR, Banffshire
Status	Campbell Distillers Ltd
Reception Centre	No
Established	1826
Age when bottled	10 years
Strength	40%

TASTING NOTES

Nose	Rich malt aroma comes through.
Taste	A hint of smoke on the palate with a restrained sweetness.
Comments	A good after-dinner dram. A well balanced Speyside, having all the characteristics in moderation.

PERSONAL NOTES

Malt	**ARDMORE**
Distillery	Ardmore KENNETHMONT, Aberdeenshire
Status	Allied Distillers Ltd
Reception Centre	No
Established	1898–9

TASTING NOTES (18 year old, 46%)

Nose	A light aroma.
Taste	Big, sweet and malty on the palate with a good, crisp finish.
Comments	Only from the independent bottlers (see page 138). After-dinner.

PERSONAL NOTES

SPEYSIDE
SINGLE MALT *SCOTCH WHISKY*

AULTMORE

distillery located between *KEITH* and *BUCKIE* began production in
1897. The name, derived from the Gaelic, means "big burn".
Ideal supplies of *water* and *peat* from the *Foggie Moss* made this area
a haunt of *illicit distillers* in the past. *Water* from the *Burn of
AUCHINDERRAN* is now used to produce this *smooth, well balanced
single MALT* ℈ *SCOTCH WHISKY* with a *mellow* finish.

AGED **12** YEARS

43% vol *Distilled & Bottled in SCOTLAND* AULTMORE DISTILLERY *Keith, Banffshire, Scotland* 70 cl

Brand	**AULTMORE**
Distillery	Aultmore KEITH, Banffshire
Status	United Distillers
Reception Centre	No
Established	1896
Age when bottled	12 years
Strength	43%

TASTING NOTES

Nose	A delighted fresh aroma with a sweet hint and a touch of peat.
Taste	Smooth, well balanced with a mellow, warming finish.
Comments	Available readily and suitable as an after-dinner malt.

PERSONAL NOTES

Brand	**BALMENACH**
Distillery	Balmenach Cromdale, GRANTOWN-ON-SPEY, Morayshire
Status	United Distillers
Reception Centre	No
Established	c1824
Age when bottled	12 years
Strength	43%

TASTING NOTE (15 year old, 46%)

Nose	Light attractive nutty aroma with a hint of smoke.
Taste	Quite full, and one does savour the malt, a good firm taste and tends to finish quickly.
Comments	A pre-dinner dram available from the independent bottlers (see page 138) or from the distillery.

PERSONAL NOTES

Malt	**THE BALVENIE**
Distillery	Balvenie DUFFTOWN, Banffshire
Status	Wm Grant & Sons Ltd
Reception Centre	No, but visitors are always welcome. Tel: 0340–20373.
Established	1892
Age when bottled	The Classic — 12 years minimum Founder's Reserve — 10 years minimum.
Strength	The Classic — 43%, Founder's Reserve — 40%, 43% for export.

TASTING NOTES

Nose	Excellent well-pronounced aroma.
Taste	Big, distinctive flavour. Almost a liqueur and a very distinct sweet aftertaste.
Comments	A connoisseur's malt for after-dinner.

PERSONAL NOTES

Malt	**BENRIACH**
Distillery	Benriach Longmorn, ELGIN, Morayshire
Status	The Seagram Co Ltd
Reception Centre	No
Established	1898

TASTING NOTES (21 year old, 46%)

Nose	Light, sweet and delicate with a hint of fruit.
Taste	A positive taste of sweetness and malt with a gentle mild fruitiness that slowly comes through on the palate.
Comments	A pre-dinner dram from the independent bottlers (see page 138).

PERSONAL NOTES

Brand	**BENRINNES**
Distillery	Benrinnes ABERLOUR, Banffshire
Status	United Distillers
Reception Centre	No
Established	c1835
Age when bottled	15 years
Strength	43%

TASTING NOTES (23 year old, 46%)

Nose	A delightful sweet and flowery aroma.
Taste	Firm, positive with a hint of blackberry fruitiness. It has a liqueur like quality with a clean fresh taste which lingers.
Comments	An excellent after-dinner dram but only available from the independent bottlers and at the distillery. (See page 138).

PERSONAL NOTES

Malt	**BENROMACH**
Distillery	Benromach FORRES, Morayshire
Status	United Distillers
Reception Centre	No
Established	1898

TASTING NOTES (14 year old, 46%)

Nose	Light, delicate and attractive.
Taste	Light and delicate but finishes with a pronounced spirit taste.
Comments	Only available from the independent bottlers (see page 138). Pre-dinner.

PERSONAL NOTES

Malt	# CAPERDONICH
Distillery	Caperdonich ROTHES, Morayshire
Status	The Seagram Co Ltd
Reception Centre	No
Established	1898

TASTING NOTES (14 year old, 46%)

Nose	A light, very delicate fragrance of peat.
Taste	Medium, slight hint of fruit with a quick smokey finish.
Comments	Only from the independent bottlers (see page 138). The distillery is across the road from Glen Grant and used to be called Glen Grant No 2.

PERSONAL NOTES

Cardhu Distillery

Brand	**CARDHU** (Kaar-doo)
Distillery	Cardhu KNOCKANDO, Morayshire
Status	United Distillers
Reception Centre	Yes. Now a major tourist attraction. Tel: 03406–204
Established	1824
Age when bottled	12 years
Strength	40%

TASTING NOTES

Nose	A hint of sweetness with an excellent bouquet.
Taste	Smooth, mellow flavour with a delightful long-lasting finish.
Comments	Good after-dinner dram, and a malt which is now one of UD's most popular.

PERSONAL NOTES

Malt	**COLEBURN**
Distillery	Coleburn Longmorn, ELGIN, Morayshire
Status	United Distillers
Reception Centre	No
Established	1897

TASTING NOTES

Nose	Light and flowery.
Taste	Light and pleasant with a well rounded refreshing aftertaste.
Comments	Only available from the independent bottlers (see page 138).

PERSONAL NOTES

Malt	**CONVALMORE**
Distillery	Convalmore DUFFTOWN, Banffshire
Status	United Distillers
Reception Centre	No
Established	1894

TASTING NOTES (27 year old, 46%)

Nose	Light, aromatic — heather aroma.
Taste	Much more on the palate than the nose suggests. A pleasant roundness and quite full, which drifts away slowly.
Comments	An after-dinner malt from the independent bottlers. (See page 138).

PERSONAL NOTES

Brand	**CRAGGANMORE**
Distillery	Cragganmore BALLINDALLOCH, Banffshire
Status	United Distillers
Reception Centre	Yes. Visiting by appointment. Tel: 08072-202
Established	1869–70
Age when bottled	12 years
Strength	40%

TASTING NOTES

Nose	Light, delicate honey nose.
Taste	A refined, well balanced distillate, quite firm with a malty smoke taste which finishes quickly.
Comments	At last available as a brand in UD's Classic Malt range.

PERSONAL NOTES

Brand	**CRAIGELLACHIE**
Distillery	Craigellachie CRAIGELLACHIE, Banffshire
Status	United Distillers
Reception Centre	No
Established	1891
Age when bottled	14 years
Strength	43%

TASTING NOTES (22 year old, 46%)

Nose	Pungent, smokey.
Taste	Light-bodied, smokey flavour. More delicate on the palate than the nose suggests. Good character.
Comments	After-dinner, but only available from the independent bottlers (see page 138) or from the distillery.

PERSONAL NOTES

Malt	**DAILUAINE**
Distillery	Dailuaine CARRON, Morayshire
Status	United Distillers
Reception Centre	No, but visitors are welcome
Established	c1852

TASTING NOTES (22 year old, 46%)

Nose	A mild sweetness which is quite gentle and resembles honeysuckle.
Taste	Robust, full bodied, fruity sweetness which really stimulates the taste buds. Has an excellent balance between refinement and positive assertion of malt.
Comments	An excellent after-dinner dram from the independent bottlers (see page 138).

PERSONAL NOTES

Malt	**DALLAS DHU**
	(*Dallas-Doo*)
Distillery	Dallas Dhu
	FORRES, Morayshire
Status	United Distillers
Reception Centre	Yes. Tel: 0309–76548
Established	1899

TASTING NOTES (21 year old, 46%)

Nose	Delicate touch of peat.
Taste	Full-bodied, lingering flavour and smooth aftertaste.
Comments	The entire distillery is now run by Historic Buildings and Monuments and is an excellent place to visit. An after-dinner dram available from the distillery and the independent bottlers (see page 138).

PERSONAL NOTES

Brand	**DUFFTOWN**
Distillery	Dufftown DUFFTOWN, Banffshire
Status	United Distillers
Reception Centre	No
Established	1896
Age when bottled	10 years
Strength	40%

TASTING NOTES

Nose	Light, flowery, pleasant aroma.
Taste	Good, round, smooth taste which tends to linger on the palate.
Comments	Pre-dinner.

PERSONAL NOTES

Brand	**GLENALLACHIE**
Distillery	Glenallachie ABERLOUR, Banffshire
Status	Campbell Distillers Ltd
Reception Centre	No
Established	1967–8
Age when bottled	12 years
Strength	40%, 43% for export

TASTING NOTES

Nose	Very elegant with a delightful bouquet.
Taste	Smooth bodied with a lovely, light sweet finish. Extremely well balanced.
Comments	Built by W Delmé-Evans for Charles Mackinlay & Co Ltd, this distillery produces one of the most under-rated malts now firmly in French hands.

PERSONAL NOTES

Brand	**GLENBURGIE**
Distillery	Glenburgie-Glenlivet FORRES, Morayshire
Status	Allied Distillers Ltd
Reception Centre	No
Established	1829
Age when bottled	5 years old, but only occasionally available.
Strength	40%

TASTING NOTES (18 year old, 46%)

Nose	A fragrant, herbal aroma.
Taste	A light, delicate, aromatic flavour with a pleasant finish.
Comments	Usually bottled for export only. A good pre-dinner malt.

PERSONAL NOTES

Brand	**GLENDRONACH**
Distillery	Glendronach Forgue, by HUNTLY, Aberdeenshire
Status	Allied Distillers Ltd
Reception Centre	Yes
Established	1826
Age when bottled	12 years (Original & Sherrywood)
Strength	40%, 43% for export

TASTING NOTES (Sherrywood)

Nose	Smooth aroma with a light trace of sweetness.
Taste	Well balanced, lingering on the palate with a delicious, decisive after-taste.
Comments	A good dram, after-dinner and much sought after.

PERSONAL NOTES

SPEYSIDE
SiNGLE MALT
SCOTCH WHISKY

GLENDULLAN

*distillery, located in a beautiful wooded
valley was built in 1897 and is one of seven
established in Dufftown in the 19th
The River Fiddich flows past the distillery;
originally providing power to drive
machinery, it is now used for cooling.
GLENDULLAN is a firm, mellow single MALT
SCOTCH WHISKY with a fruity
bouquet and a smooth lingering finish.*

AGED **12** YEARS

43% vol   70 cl

Distilled & Bottled in SCOTLAND
GLENDULLAN DISTILLERY
Dufftown, Keith, Banffshire, Scotland

Brand	**GLENDULLAN**
Distillery	Glendullan DUFFTOWN, Banffshire
Status	United Distillers
Reception Centre	Tel: 0340–20250
Established	1897–8
Age when bottled	12 years
Strength	43%

TASTING NOTES

Nose	Attractive, fruity bouquet.
Taste	Firm, mellow with a delightful finish and a smooth lingering aftertaste.
Comments	Not very well known, but a good after-dinner malt.

PERSONAL NOTES

WHITE HORSE
GLEN ELGIN
SINGLE HIGHLAND MALT
SCOTCH WHISKY

DISTILLED AND BOTTLED IN SCOTLAND
WHITE HORSE DISTILLERS, GLASGOW, SCOTLAND
ウイスキー

750 ml   GLEN ELGIN DISTILLERY, ELGIN, MORAYSHIRE   43% vol

Brand	**GLEN ELGIN**
Distillery	Glen Elgin Longmorn, ELGIN, Morayshire
Status	United Distillers
Reception Centre	No
Established	1898–1900
Age when bottled	12 years
Strength	43%

TASTING NOTES

Nose	Agreeable aroma of heather and honey.
Taste	Medium-weight touch of sweetness which finishes smoothly.
Comments	The best of both worlds, an excellent all-round malt, suitable for drinking at any time.

PERSONAL NOTES

Brand	**GLENFARCLAS**
Distillery	Glenfarclas Marypark, BALLINDALLOCH, Banffshire
Status	J & G Grant
Reception Centre	Tel: 08072–257 ext. 213
Established	1836
Age when bottled	8, 10, 12, 15, 21 & 25 years
Strength	8 year old — 60% ('105') 10 year old — 40% 15 year old — 46% 12 (export), 21 & 25 year old — 43%

TASTING NOTES (15 year old, 46%)

Nose	A rich, delicious promise (which is fulfilled).
Taste	Full of character and flavour. One of the great Highland malts.
Comments	The 60% vol (105°) is an interesting experience, however, not to be undertaken by the unwary! Quoted in the Guinness Book of Records.

PERSONAL NOTES

Brand	**GLENFIDDICH**
Distillery	Glenfiddich DUFFTOWN, Banffshire
Status	Wm Grant & Sons Ltd
Reception Centre	Yes, very popular. Tel: 0340–20373
Established	1886–7
Age when bottled	8 years minimum
Strength	40%

TASTING NOTES

Nose	A light, delicate touch of peat.
Taste	Attractive flavour, with an after-sweetness. Well balanced. A good introductory malt.
Comments	If you have never tasted a malt, start with this one.

PERSONAL NOTES

Brand	**GLENGLASSAUGH**
Distillery	Glenglassaugh PORTSOY, Banffshire
Status	The Highland Distilleries Co plc
Reception Centre	No
Established	1875
Age when bottled	12 years old
Strength	40%

TASTING NOTES

Nose	Light, fresh and delicate.
Taste	Charming, a hint of sweetness which is full of promise with a delicious stimulating foliow-through.
Comments	For drinking at anytime. Good to see Highland branding it.

PERSONAL NOTES

Brand	**GLEN GRANT**
Distillery	Glen Grant ROTHES, Morayshire
Status	The Seagram Co Ltd
Reception Centre	Yes. Tel: 03403–494
Established	1840
Age when bottled	UK market — none given. Export market — 5 years old (Italy), 10 years old and none given
Strength	40%

TASTING NOTES

Nose	Light, dry aroma.
Taste	Dry flavour, light — another good all-round malt.
Comments	Pre-dinner. Hugely popular in Italy.

PERSONAL NOTES

Malt	**GLEN KEITH**
Distillery	Glen Keith KEITH, Banffshire
Status	The Seagram Co Ltd
Reception Centre	No
Established	1957–60

TASTING NOTES *(22 year old, 45.6%)*

Nose	A light, dry hint of sweetness with undertones of smoke.
Taste	As with the aroma it has a light, fruity sweetness which results in a smooth well balanced palate.
Comments	Due to its overall lightness both in aroma and taste it is a good pre-dinner dram from the independent bottlers (see page 138)

PERSONAL NOTES

Brand	**GLENLIVET**
Distillery	Glenlivet MINMORE, Banffshire
Status	The Seagram Co Ltd
Reception Centre	Yes. Tel: 08073–427
Established	1858
Age when bottled	12 years
Strength	40%, 43% for export

TASTING NOTES

Nose	A light, delicate nose with lots of fruit.
Taste	Medium-light trace of sweetness, quite full on the palate — a first class malt.
Comments	This one never disappoints. Popular and available everywhere.

PERSONAL NOTES

Malt	**GLENLOSSIE**
Distillery	Glenlossie-Glenlivet ELGIN, Morayshire
Status	United Distillers
Reception Centre	No
Established	1876

TASTING NOTES (24 year old, 46%)

Nose	A soft touch of sweetness with sandalwood overtones.
Taste	Has mellowed with age and has a long lasting smoothness with an almond-like finish.
Comments	An after dinner dram only available from the independent bottlers (see page 138).

PERSONAL NOTES

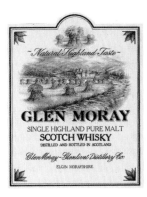

Brand	**GLEN MORAY**
Distillery	Glen Moray ELGIN, Morayshire
Status	Subsidiary of Macdonald Martin Distillers plc
Reception Centre	No
Established	1897
Age when bottled	12 years
Strength	40%

TASTING NOTES

Nose	Fresh, light aroma.
Taste	Light, pleasant and malty with a clean finish. A fine all-round malt.
Comments	A pre-dinner dram, beautifully presented.

PERSONAL NOTES

Brand	**THE GLEN ROTHES**
Distillery	Glenrothes ROTHES, Morayshire
Status	The Highland Distilleries Co plc
Reception Centre	No
Established	1878
Age when bottled	12 years old
Strength	43%

TASTING NOTES

Nose	A rich subtle sweetness with a lingering hint of peat-reek.
Taste	A good balance of softness and quality with an exquisite long-lasting flavour.
Comments	After dinner and now available from Berry Bros & Rudd Ltd of *Cutty Sark* fame.

PERSONAL NOTES

Brand	**GLEN SPEY**
Distillery	Glen Spey ROTHES, Morayshire
Status	International Distillers & Vintners Ltd
Reception Centre	No
Established	c1878
Age when bottled	8 years
Strength	40%

TASTING NOTES

Nose	Light, fragrant and delicate.
Taste	Very smooth and fragrant. A good all-round drink.
Comments	Pre-dinner.

PERSONAL NOTES

Malt	**GLENTAUCHERS**
Distillery	Glentauchers MULBEN, Banffshire
Status	Allied Distillers Ltd
Reception Centre	No
Established	1898

TASTING NOTES (20 year old, 46%)

Nose	Light, sweet aroma.
Taste	Lightly flavoured with a light, dry finish.
Comments	A pre-dinner dram from the independent bottlers (see page 139).

PERSONAL NOTES

Malt	**IMPERIAL**
Distillery	Imperial CARRON, Morayshire
Status	Allied Distillers Ltd
Reception Centre	No
Established	1897

TASTING NOTES (1969 distillation)

Nose	Delightful — rich and smokey.
Taste	Rich and mellow with an absolutely delicious finish. A malt of real character.
Comments	After-dinner, again only from the independent bottlers (see page 139). Very rare at the moment.

PERSONAL NOTES

Brand	**INCHGOWER**
Distillery	Inchgower BUCKIE, Banffshire
Status	United Distillers
Reception Centre	Provisional
Established	1871
Age when bottled	12 years
Strength	40%

TASTING NOTES

Nose	Very distinctive with a pleasant hint of sweetness.
Taste	Good, distinctive flavour finishing with a light sweetness.
Comments	A well balanced malt. After-dinner.

PERSONAL NOTES

Brand	**KNOCKANDO**
Distillery	Knockando KNOCKANDO, Morayshire
Status	The International Distillers & Vintners Ltd
Reception Centre	No
Established	1898
Age when bottled	10–15 years
Strength	40%

TASTING NOTES

Nose	Full pleasant aroma of hot butter.
Taste	Medium-bodied with a pleasant syrupy flavour which finishes quite quickly.
Comments	After-dinner. Bottled when it is considered ready, rather than at a pre-determined age. The label carries dates of distillation and bottling.

PERSONAL NOTES

Brand	**KNOCKDHU** (*Knock-doo*)
Distillery	Knockdhu KNOCK, Banffshire
Status	Inver House Distillers Ltd
Reception Centre	No
Established	1893–4
Age when bottled	12 years
Strength	40%

TASTING NOTES

Nose	A distinctive soft aroma with a hint of smoke.
Taste	So surprisingly refined with a mellow, smooth, mild softness and a good long finish.
Comments	An excellent all round malt. This distillery was the first built by The Distillers Co to supply malt whisky for their own use. A great welcome back.

PERSONAL NOTES

SPEYSIDE
SINGLE MALT
SCOTCH WHISKY

LINKWOOD

*distillery stands on the River Lossie,
close to ELGIN in Speyside. The distillery
has retained its traditional atmosphere
since its establishment in 1821.
Great care & has always
been taken to safeguard the
character of the whisky which has
remained the same through the
years. Linkwood is one of the
FINEST & Single Malt Scotch Whiskies
available - full bodied with a hint of
sweetness and a slightly smoky aroma.*

YEARS 12 OLD

43% vol   Bottled & Bottled in SCOTLAND
LINKWOOD DISTILLERY
Elgin, Moray, Scotland   70cl

Brand	**LINKWOOD**
Distillery	Linkwood ELGIN, Morayshire
Status	United Distillers
Reception centre	No. Visiting by appointment Tel: 0343–547004
Established	c1824
Age when bottled	12 years
Strength	43%

TASTING NOTES

Nose	Slightly smokey with a trace of sweetness.
Taste	Full-bodied hint of sweetness.
Comments	One of the best malts available.

PERSONAL NOTES

Brand	**LONGMORN**
Distillery	Longmorn Longmorn, ELGIN, Morayshire
Status	The Seagram Co Ltd
Reception Centre	No
Established	1894-5
Age when bottled	15 years
Strength	43%

TASTING NOTES

Nose	A delicious full fragrant bouquet of spirit.
Taste	Full bodied, fleshy, nutty and surprisingly refined.
Comments	Re-introduced at this age in 1986 by marketers Hill, Thomson & Co — at last the public can appreciate this classic after-dinner malt. Outstanding.

PERSONAL NOTES

Brand	**THE MACALLAN**
Distillery	Macallan CRAIGELLACHIE, Banffshire
Status	The Macallan Distillers Ltd
Reception centre	Yes. By appointment only.
Established	c1824
Age when bottled	UK market — 10, 18 (currently 1972 distillation) and 25 years old. Export market — 10, 12, 18, and 25 years old. Italian market — 7 years old.
Strength	7 and 10 year old — 40%, with some 10 year old at 57%; 25 year old, 1968 distillation and export bottlings — 43%.

TASTING NOTES (10 year old, 40%)

Nose	Smooth aroma with a silky bouquet.
Taste	Full, delightful and sherried with a beautiful lingering after-taste.
Comments	A masterpiece. All Macallan is casked in sherrywood.

PERSONAL NOTES

Brand	**MILTON DUFF**
Distillery	Miltonduff-Glenlivet ELGIN, Morayshire
Status	Allied Distillers Ltd
Reception Centre	Yes. Tel: 0343–547433
Established	1824
Age when bottled	12 years
Strength	43%

TASTING NOTES

Nose	Agreeable, fragrant bouquet.
Taste	Medium bodied with a pleasant, well matured, subtle finish.
Comments	After-dinner. Another malt called *Mosstowie* used to be produced from Lomond type stills at Milton Duff and is available from the independent bottlers (see page 139).

PERSONAL NOTES

SPEYSIDE
SINGLE MALT
SCOTCH WHISKY

MORTLACH

was the first of seven
distilleries in Dufftown. In the
C19th farm animals kept in
adjoining byres were fed on
barley left over from processing.
Today water from springs in
the CONVAL HILLS is used to
produce this delightful
smooth, fruity single
MALT SCOTCH WHISKY.

AGED 16 YEARS

Distilled & Bottled in SCOTLAND
MORTLACH DISTILLERY
Dufftown, Keith, Banffshire, Scotland

43% vol   70 cl

Brand	**MORTLACH**
Distillery	Mortlach DUFFTOWN, Banffshire
Status	United Distillers
Reception centre	No
Established	c1823
Age when bottled	16 years
Strength	43%

TASTING NOTES (12 year old, 40%)

Nose	A pleasant, well-rounded aroma.
Taste	Medium-bodied with a well balanced delightful finish.
Comments	A first class after-dinner malt from the independent bottlers (see page 139) and the distillery.

PERSONAL NOTES

Malt	# PITTYVAICH
Distillery	Pittyvaich DUFFTOWN, Banffshire
Status	United Distillers
Reception Centre	No
Established	1974

TASTING NOTES (1976 distillation, 57.7%)

Nose	Rather elegant with a delicate fragrance.
Taste	Mellow and soft with a fulfilling roundness.
Comments	A remarkably good addition to the bottled malts. After dinner, but only available from the independent bottlers (see page 139).

PERSONAL NOTES

Auchroisk Distillery

Brand	**THE SINGLETON OF AUCHROISK**
Distillery	Auchroisk MULBEN, Banffshire
Status	International Distillers & Vintners Ltd
Reception centre	No
Established	1974
Age when bottled	12 years minimum
Strength	40%, 43% for export

TASTING NOTES

Nose	Distinctive, attractive bouquet with a touch of fruit.
Taste	Medium-weight, hint of sweetness with a delicious long-lasting flavour.
Comments	After-dinner. It has really gathered a substantial following during its first few years on the market.

PERSONAL NOTES

SPEYSIDE
SINGLE MALT
SCOTCH WHISKY

SPEYBURN

is an unusually compact distillery. Owing
to its hilly location, on the outskirts of
ROTHES, it comprises buildings two
and three storeys high. Established in
1897 it was the first malt distillery to
install a mechanical making & system
consisting of moving drums. Water
from the GRANTY BURN is used to
produce this light, sweet single MALT
SCOTCH WHISKY with an oaky finish.

AGED **12** YEARS

43% vol   70cl

Brand	**SPEYBURN**
Distillery	Speyburn ROTHES, Morayshire
Status	United Distillers
Reception Centre	No
Established	1897
Age when bottled	12 years
Strength	43%

TASTING NOTES (16 year old, 46%)

Nose	A heather-honey bouquet.
Taste	Big, full-bodied malty taste with a sweet finish.
Comments	After-dinner. From the independent bottlers only (see page 139) or the distillery.

PERSONAL NOTES

Brand	**STRATHISLA** (*Strath-eyela*)
Distillery	Strathisla KEITH, Banffshire
Status	The Seagram Co Ltd
Reception centre	Yes. Tel: 05422–7471.
Established	1786
Age when bottled	12 years
Strength	40%

TASTING NOTES

Nose	Beautiful, bewitching fragrance of fruit which also reflects the taste to come.
Taste	Slender hint of sweetness with an extremely long, lingering fullness. Good balance.
Comments	An excellent after-dinner malt — one of the best to sip and savour. Distilled and bottled by Chivas Brothers Ltd.

PERSONAL NOTES

Brand	**TAMDHU** (*Tamm-doo*)
Distillery	Tamdhu KNOCKANDO, Morayshire
Status	The Highland Distilleries Co plc
Reception Centre	Yes. Tel: 03406–221
Established	1896–7
Age when bottled	10 years
Strength	40%

TASTING NOTES

Nose	Light aroma with a trace of sweetness.
Taste	Medium, with a little sweetness and a very mellow finish.
Comments	A good after-dinner dram which is both popular and readily available.

PERSONAL NOTES

Brand	**TAMNAVULIN**
	(*Tamna-voolin*)
Distillery	Tamnavulin
	BALLINDALLOCH, Banffshire
Status	The Invergordon Distillers Ltd
Reception centre	Yes. A charming old mill with a beautiful sheltered picnic area Tel: 08073–442
Established	1965–6
Age when bottled	10 years, 15 for Italy
Strength	40%, 43%

TASTING NOTES

Nose	Well matured with a distinct mellowness and a hint of sweetness.
Taste	Medium weight with a light, smokey, pronounced finish.
Comments	A good all-round malt.

PERSONAL NOTES

Brand	**TOMINTOUL-GLENLIVET** *(Tommin-towl)*
Distillery	Tomintoul-Glenlivet BALLINDALLOCH, Banffshire
Status	Whyte & Mackay Distillers Ltd
Reception Centre	Tel: 08073–274
Established	1964–5
Age when bottled	8, 12 years
Strength	40%, 43% for export

TASTING NOTES (12 year old, 40%)

Nose	Light and delicate.
Taste	Light body with good character.
Comments	A good introduction to malt. Bottled in an interesting manner for export.

PERSONAL NOTES

Brand	**THE TORMORE**
Distillery	Tormore Advie, GRANTOWN-ON-SPEY, Morayshire
Status	Allied Distillers Ltd
Reception centre	No, but visitors are welcome. Tel: 0807–5244
Established	1958–60
Age when bottled	10 years, and 5 for Italy
Strength	40%, up to 43% for export

TASTING NOTES

Nose	Nicely defined dry aroma.
Taste	Medium-bodied with a hint of sweetness and a pleasant, lingering aftertaste.
Comments	After-dinner.

PERSONAL NOTES

THE HIGHLANDS

Outwith the Speyside area distilling activity is spread more sparsely throughout a wide area which I have taken the liberty to break up into four main regions in the North, South, East and West.

Over 30 malts emanate from these four areas, some sadly from distilleries no longer in existence such as Glen Mhor and Glen Albyn in Inverness, and Glenugie near Peterhead. When you do come across an example of these, remember that you really will be buying a piece of history.

In the far-flung producing localities around the Highlands the importance of the visitor is often keenly felt and despite the travel required to reach these facilities, Highland hospitality still abounds. The existing distilleries in the Northern region stretch from Dalwhinnie near Kingussie to Pulteney at Wick in the north of Caithness and encompass Tomatin at the hamlet of the same name; Royal Brackla near Nairn; Millburn in Inverness; Ord Distillery at Muir of Ord in the Black Isle; Dalmore and Teaninich at Alness; Balblair and Glenmorangie near Tain and Clynelish near Brora. Although most of these malts are not as well known as they should be, many are becoming more popular and none of them should be passed by if you come across them.

The Eastern malts lie between the generalised Speyside region and the North Sea coast. Banff, the fishing town on the Moray Firth possesses two distilleries, though only Glen Deveron is currently in production. The distillery with the town's name has been "mothballed" for some time and the availability of the malt has fluctuated in the recent past. Although Glenugie distillery is defunct, the Peterhead malt can still be found in many specialist shops.

Farming has made the lush lowland area around Aberdeen famous, so it is no surprise to

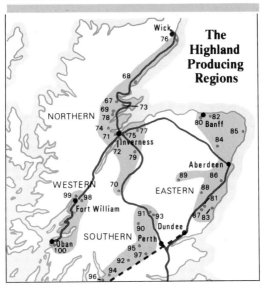

The Highland Producing Regions

Wick 76
68
67
69
73
NORTHERN
78
82
80 Banff
85
74
77
71 75
Inverness
84
72
79
Aberdeen
89
86
WESTERN
70
88
99 98
EASTERN
81
Fort William
91 93
87 83
90 Dundee
SOUTHERN Perth
Oban 95
100 97
92
94
96

Distillery location numbers refer to page numbers.

find that at Glen Garioch waste heat from the
direct-fired stills is used to cultivate tomatoes and
pot plants. And while Lochnagar cannot offer the
visitor such horticultural delights, its new reception
centre and proximity to Balmoral Castle make it not
only Royal, but a bit special. To the south of
Deeside Glenury Royal near Stonehaven and
Fettercairn extend the activity to Montrose which
boasts a considerable amount of distilling. Glenesk
distillery has changed names a few times but its malt
remains the same whereas Lochside Distillery (once
a brewery) produces both grain and malt whisky.
Lochside is very rare and only available from the
independent bottlers. Inland, but still on the South
Esk river, Brechin has two distillieries at Glencadam
and North Port — again both producing quite rare
malts. South of this arable region the hills of
Perthshire signal the Southern limits of the
Highland distilling area.

At Pitlochry, the gateway to the Highlands, the

malt drinker can experience two contrasting distilleries. Edradour is the smallest in Scotland and yet maintains all the advantages of a small 19th century plant, while Blair Athol is a large modern distillery with a new reception centre and retail outlet. Aberfeldy Distillery lies at the eastern entrance to the town of the same name on the banks of the River Tay and Glenturret Distillery at Crieff caters for the visitor as well as any distillery can. Tullibardine at Blackford is a ''recent'' distillery (1948) in a village which also has a mineral water producer and the only commercial malting floors in Scotland built on arguably the oldest brewery site in Scotland! And if that amount of diversity is a surprise, Deanston Distillery on the River Teith at Doune is a converted cotton mill where the vaulted weaving sheds act as bonded warehouses and a small hydro-electric generating station is also situated within the plant itself! In the far west of this most southerly of the Highland regions lie Loch Lomond and Glengoyne distilleries. Both almost straddle the Highland line (as does Tullibardine) but claim allegiance to the Highland region. Loch Lomond is a relatively new distillery (1968) which currently produces Inchmurrin malt, whereas Glengoyne has a longer pedigree and resting in a cleft of the Campsie Fells, uniquely caters for visitors with guided tours, retail outlet and a bar with a balcony overlooking a rock pool.

The Western malts are an altogether rarer breed being only three in number. Oban's distillery is situated just off the High Street of this thriving tourist town and is therefore somewhat stretched for visitor facilities, but up the coast at Fort William the mothballed Glenlochy Distillery occupies a site which makes one wonder why the owners have not put it to use attracting tourists. Ben Nevis Distillery on the north of the town is back in production and is aptly named considering the breathtaking backdrop.

THE NORTHERN HIGHLANDS

Brand	**BALBLAIR**
Distillery	Balblair Edderton, TAIN, Ross-shire
Status	Allied Distillers Ltd
Reception centre	No
Established	1790
Age when bottled	5, 10 years
Strength	40%

TASTING NOTES (5 year old, 40%)

Nose	Pronounced and distinctive fragrance of smoke and sweetness.
Taste	Good lingering flavour, long-lasting with a slender hint of sweetness.
Comments	A fine dram anytime. Now bottled by Ballantines and available on the UK market. Has just celebrated its 200th birthday.

PERSONAL NOTES

SINGLE MALT
SCOTCH WHISKY

One of the most northerly in Scotland,

CLYNELISH

*distillery, was established in Brora
by the Marquess of STAFFORD
in 1819. Its building signalled the
end of illicit distilling
in the area and provided a
ready market for locally grown
barley. Water is piped from the
CLYNEMILTON burn to produce this
fruity, & slightly smoky single
MALT SCOTCH WHISKY much
appreciated by connoisseurs*

YEARS **14** OLD

43% vol   70cl

Brand	**CLYNELISH** (*Kline-leesh*)
Distillery	Clynelish BRORA, Sutherland
Status	United Distillers
Reception Centre	No. Visiting by appointment. Tel: 0408–2144
Established	1967–8
Age when bottled	14 years
Strength	43%

TASTING NOTES

Nose	Quite peaty for a Northern malt.
Taste	Rich, pleasant with a slightly dry finish — lots of character.
Comments	Good after-dinner malt. Popular amongst the connoisseurs.

PERSONAL NOTES

Brand	**DALMORE**
Distillery	Dalmore ALNESS, Ross-shire
Status	Whyte & Mackay Distillers Ltd
Reception centre	No
Established	c1839
Age when bottled	12 years
Strength	40%, 43% for export

TASTING NOTES

Nose	Rich, fresh, with a suggestion of sweetness.
Taste	Full flavour which finishes a touch dry.
Comments	Another really good malt. After-dinner.

PERSONAL NOTES

Brand	**DALWHINNIE**
Distillery	Dalwhinnie DALWHINNIE, Inverness-shire
Status	United Distillers UK
Reception centre	Yes. Just opened. Tel: 05282–264
Established	1897–8
Age when bottled	15 years
Strength	43%

TASTING NOTES

Nose	A gentle aromatic bouquet.
Taste	A luscious flavour with a light honey sweet finish.
Comments	Pre-dinner, and part of UD's Classic Malt range.

PERSONAL NOTES

Malt	**GLEN ALBYN**
Distillery	Glen Albyn INVERNESS, Inverness-shire (Dismantled 1986)
Status	c1846

TASTING NOTES (20 year old, 46%)

Nose	Light and smokey. Pleasant.
Taste	Well-rounded, smokey with a full finish.
Comments	Only available from the independent bottlers (see page 138).

PERSONAL NOTES

Dalwhinnie Distillery

Malt	**GLEN MHOR** (*Glen Vawr*)
Distillery	Glen Mhor INVERNESS, Inverness-shire (Dismantled 1986)
Established	1892

TASTING NOTES (8 year old, 40%)

Nose	Light, sweet fragrance.
Taste	Light-bodied with a slightly dry finish.
Comments	Good, all-round drinking from the independent bottlers (see page 139).

PERSONAL NOTES

Brand	**GLENMORANGIE**
Distillery	Glenmorangie TAIN, Ross-shire
Status	Subsidiary of Macdonald Martin Distillers plc
Reception Centre	No
Established	1843
Age when bottled	10, 18 years old
Strength	40% and cask strength

TASTING NOTES (10 year old, 40%)

Nose	Beautiful aroma. Fresh and sweet with a subtle hint of peat.
Taste	Medium-bodied with a sweet, fresh finish. One to linger and dwell upon.
Comments	An excellent malt, very popular. Now available at cask strength too. Entire distillery output is sold as single bottled malt.

PERSONAL NOTES

Brand	**GLENORDIE** *(formerly ORD)*
Distillery	Ord MUIR of ORD, Ross-shire
Status	United Distillers
Reception centre	Yes. Tel: 0463–870421
Established	1838
Age when bottled	12 years
Strength	40%

TASTING NOTES

Nose	A beautifully deep nose, with a tinge of dryness.
Taste	Good depth with a long-lasting, delicious aftertaste. Very smooth.
Comments	After-dinner.

PERSONAL NOTES

Malt	**MILLBURN**
Distillery	Millburn INVERNESS, Inverness-shire
Status	United Distillers
Reception Centre	No
Established	c1807

TASTING NOTES (13 year old, 46%)

Nose	A rich aroma with a faint sweetness.
Taste	Full-bodied, a touch of fruit and a good long finish.
Comments	Only from the independent bottlers (see page 139).

PERSONAL NOTES

Malt	**OLD PULTENEY**
	(Pult-nay)
Distillery	Pulteney
	WICK, Caithness
Status	Allied Distillers Ltd
Reception centre	No
Established	1826

TASTING NOTES (8 year old, 40%)

Nose	Fine, delicate, light aroma with a hint of the Island malts.
Taste	Light, crisp and refreshing with a hint of fullness which gives a positive finish of length.
Comments	An excellent aperitif whisky but only available from the independent bottlers (see page 139). The most northerly mainland distillery.

PERSONAL NOTES

Malt	ROYAL BRACKLA
Distillery	Royal Brackla NAIRN, Morayshire
Status	United Distillers
Reception Centre	No
Established	c1812

TASTING NOTES (18 year old, 46%)

Nose	A complex balance of peat and smoke with a touch of sweetness.
Taste	Big, and the peaty-smokey nose comes through on the palate with a hint of fruit and a dry finish.
Comments	United Distillers have announced they are re-opening this distillery. From the independent bottlers (see page 139).

PERSONAL NOTES

Malt	**TEANINICH**
Distillery	Teaninich ALNESS, Ross-shire
Status	United Distillers
Reception centre	No
Established	1817

TASTING NOTES (26 year old, 46%)

Nose	Subtle, fruity with a gentle bouquet.
Taste	Soft, full of flavour and a delight to drink. Really warms the palate.
Comments	A good pre-dinner malt from the independent bottlers (see page 139).

PERSONAL NOTES

Brand	**TOMATIN**
Distillery	Tomatin TOMATIN, Inverness-shire
Status	Subsidiary of Takara Shuzo & Okura & Co Ltd
Reception centre	Yes. Tel: 08082–234
Established	1897
Age when bottled	10 years
Strength	40%, 43% for export

TASTING NOTES

Nose	Pleasant and light.
Taste	Light body, very smooth.
Comments	A pre-dinner dram and a good introduction to malt whisky. The distillery was the first to be acquired by the Japanese in 1985.

PERSONAL NOTES

THE EASTERN HIGHLANDS

Malt	**BANFF**
Distillery	Banff BANFF, Banffshire
Status	United Distillers
Reception centre	No
Established	1863

TASTING NOTES (15 year old, 46%)

Nose	Very light with a trace of smoke.
Taste	Slightly aggressive, finishing a touch fiery. Nonetheless a good bite.
Comments	Available only from the independent bottlers (see page 138). A very rare dram. Distillery has been closed since 1983.

PERSONAL NOTES

Malt	**GLENCADAM**
Distillery	Glencadam BRECHIN, Angus
Status	Allied Distillers Ltd
Reception centre	Tel: 03562–2217
Established	c1825

TASTING NOTES (14 year old, 46%)

Nose	Light hint of sweetness.
Taste	Full, with quite a fruity flavour and a good finish.
Comments	An after-dinner malt which is only available from the independent bottlers (see page 139).

PERSONAL NOTES

Brand	**GLEN DEVERON**
Distillery	Macduff BANFF, Banffshire
Status	Subsidiary of General Beverage Corporation, Luxembourg
Reception centre	No
Established	1962–3
Age when bottled	12
Strength	40%

TASTING NOTES

Nose	A pronounced refreshing bouquet.
Taste	Medium weight and a smooth pleasant flavour and a clean finish.
Comments	After-dinner dram. Also available from the independent bottlers as *Macduff* (see page 139).

PERSONAL NOTES

GLENESK

YEARS 12 OLD
SINGLE MALT
HIGHLAND SCOTCH WHISKY

Wm Sanderson Son. Ltd.
Distillers, South Queensferry, Scotland
Bottled in Scotland
40% vol   75 cl

Brand	**GLEN ESK**
Distillery	Glen Esk Hillside, MONTROSE, Angus
Status	United Distillers
Reception centre	No
Established	1897
Age when bottled	12 years
Strength	40%

TASTING NOTES

Nose	A light, delicate hint of sweetness.
Taste	Quite full and sweet with a lingering finish, well balanced.
Comments	After-dinner. The distillery was once known as North Esk and also as Hillside.

PERSONAL NOTES

Brand	**GLEN GARIOCH** (*Glen-geerie*)
Distillery	Glen Garioch OLDMELDRUM, Aberdeenshire
Status	Morrison Bowmore Distillers Ltd
Reception centre	Temporarily closed
Established	1798
Age when bottled	21 years
Strength	43%

TASTING NOTES *(21 year old)*

Nose	Delicate and smokey.
Taste	Pronounced, peaty flavour with a smooth pleasant finish.
Comments	Good after-dinner dram, from a distillery which utilises waste heat to cultivate tomatoes and pot-plants.

PERSONAL NOTES

Malt	**GLENUGIE**
Distillery	Glenugie PETERHEAD, Aberdeenshire (no longer licensed)
Established	c1831

TASTING NOTES (20 year old, 46%)

Nose	Hint of ripe fruit.
Taste	Initial taste of sweetness, firm, malty but with a quick, dry finish.
Comments	Pre-dinner, from the independent bottlers (see page 139).

PERSONAL NOTES

GLENURY-ROYAL
Highland Malt
SCOTCH WHISKY

12 YEARS
SINGLE
MALT
40% Vol

12 YEARS
SINGLE
MALT
75 Cl.

100% SCOTCH WHISKY 100%
DISTILLED AND BOTTLED IN SCOTLAND
JOHN GILLON & COMPANY LTD.
Stonehaven and Glasgow
EST. 1817
PRODUCT OF SCOTLAND

Brand	**GLENURY-ROYAL**
Distillery	Glenury-Royal STONEHAVEN, Kincardineshire
Status	United Distillers
Reception centre	No
Established	c1825
Age when bottled	12 years
Strength	40%

TASTING NOTES

Nose	A light hint of smoke with a dry aroma.
Taste	Light body with a dry, smokey finish.
Comments	A good introductory malt, suitable for pre-dinner drinking.

PERSONAL NOTES

Malt	**NORTH PORT**
Distillery	North Port BRECHIN, Angus
Status	United Distillers
Reception centre	No
Established	c1820

TASTING NOTES (17 year old, 46%)

Nose	A rather sharp, pronounced aroma, almost like a pickle.
Taste	Starts sweet, but quickly fades to spirit — quite a sharp tang.
Comments	Pre-dinner, and preferably with water. Available only from the independent bottlers (see page 139) Distillery is still closed.

PERSONAL NOTES

Lochnagar Distillery

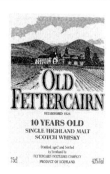

Brand	**OLD FETTERCAIRN**
Distillery	Fettercairn FETTERCAIRN, Kincardineshire
Status	White & Mackay Distillers Ltd
Reception centre	Yes. Tel: 05614–244
Established	c1824
Age when bottled	None given
Strength	40%

TASTING NOTES

Nose	Light, stimulating fresh aroma.
Taste	Fresh, slightly dry finish which is quite stimulating but gently restrained.
Comments	A good all-round drink. Reputed to be the second distillery licensed after the legislation of 1823.

PERSONAL NOTES

Brand	## ROYAL LOCHNAGAR
Distillery	Lochnagar Crathie, BALLATER, Aberdeenshire
Status	United Distillers
Reception centre	Yes, one of the best. Tel: 03397–42273
Established	1826
Age when bottled	12 years and no age given
Strength	40% and 43%

TASTING NOTES (12 year old, 40%)

Nose	Pleasant, full nose.
Taste	Good body with a full, malt-fruit-like taste and a delicious trace of sweetness.
Comments	ROYAL LOCHNAGAR SELECTED RESERVE is a special bottling available from time to time at 43%. Expect to pay around £100!

PERSONAL NOTES

THE SOUTHERN HIGHLANDS

HIGHLAND
SINGLE MALT
SCOTCH WHISKY

ABERFELDY

distillery was established in 1898 on the *road* to *Perth* and south *side* of the *RIVER TAY*. Fresh *spring water* is taken from the nearby *PITILIE burn* and used to produce this *UNIQUE single MALT SCOTCH WHISKY* with its *distinctive* PEATY nose.

AGED **15** YEARS

Distilled & Bottled in SCOTLAND
ABERFELDY DISTILLERY
Aberfeldy, Perthshire, Scotland
43% vol 70cl

Brand	**ABERFELDY**
Distillery	Aberfeldy ABERFELDY, Perthshire
Status	United Distillers
Reception centre	Yes. Tel: 0887–20330
Established	c1830
Age when bottled	15 years
Strength	43%

TASTING NOTES (1969 distillation)

Nose	Fresh clean with a lightly peated nose.
Taste	Nice substantial flavour with a good round taste.
Comments	From the independent bottlers (see page 138) and the distillery.

PERSONAL NOTES

Brand	**BLAIR ATHOL**
Distillery	Blair Athol PITLOCHRY, Perthshire
Status	United Distillers
Reception centre	Yes, with good facilities for trade and public. Tel: 0796–2234
Established	1798
Age when bottled	8 years
Strength	40%

TASTING NOTES

Nose	Light, fresh, clean aroma.
Taste	Medium hint of peat with a round finish. Plenty of flavour.
Comments	Pre-dinner, readily available.

PERSONAL NOTES

Brand	**DEANSTON**
Distillery	Deanston DOUNE, Perthshire
Status	Burn Stewart Distillers plc
Reception centre	No
Established	1965–6
Age when bottled	None given
Strength	40%

TASTING NOTES

Nose	A hint of sweetness.
Taste	Light, finishing with a smooth trace of the same.
Comments	A pre-dinner malt, from a distillery which used to be a cotton mill until 1965 and boasts not only vaulted bonds, which were formerly the weaving sheds, but also its own hydro-electric generating station! Now under new ownership.

PERSONAL NOTES

Brand	**EDRADOUR** (*Edra-Dower*)
Distillery	Edradour PITLOCHRY, Perthshire
Status	Campbell Distillers Ltd
Reception centre	Yes. Tel: 0796–2095
Established	c1837
Age when bottled	10 years
Strength	40%

TASTING NOTES (18 year old, 46%)

Nose	Fruity-sweet and smokey.
Taste	Strong marzipan taste which comes through smooth, slightly dry and malty with a nutty almond-like aftertaste.
Comments	Scotland's smallest distillery and therefore closest to a working 19th century distillery. Well worth a visit to see how it used to be done.

PERSONAL NOTES

Brand	**GLENGOYNE**
Distillery	Glengoyne DUMGOYNE, Stirlingshire
Status	Lang Brothers Ltd
Reception centre	Yes. Tel: 041–332–6361
Established	c1833
Age when bottled	10, 12 & 17 years
Strength	10 year old — 40% 12 year old — (Export & Duty Free) — 43% 17 year old — 43%

TASTING NOTES (10 year old)

Nose	A light, fresh aroma.
Taste	Light, pleasant all-round malt.
Comments	Another great introduction to malts. The 17 year old is impressive.

PERSONAL NOTES

Brand	**THE GLENTURRET**
Distillery	Glenturret The Hosh, CRIEFF, Perthshire
Status	The Highland Distilleries Co plc
Reception centre	Yes. Very popular Award Winning Heritage Centre with audio-visual, Exhibition Museum, tasting bar and restaurant.
Established	1775
Age when bottled	8, 12, 15 and 21 years
Strength	40%

TASTING NOTES (12 year old)

Nose	Very impressive aromatic nose.
Taste	Full, lush body with a good depth of flavour and a stimulating finish. Delightful.
Comments	An award-winning malt from arguably Scotland's oldest distillery.

PERSONAL NOTES

Brand	**INCHMURRIN**
Distillery	Loch Lomond ALEXANDRIA, Dunbartonshire
Status	Glen Catrine Bonded Warehouse Ltd
Reception centre	No
Established	1965–6
Age when bottled	None given
Strength	40%

TASTING NOTES

Nose	Slightly aromatic. Follows through on the palate.
Taste	Light bodied. Most of the flavour is on the front of the palate and thus finishes quickly.
Comments	A good everyday drinking malt. Pre-dinner. Formerlly owned by ADP and then Inver House Distillers, the distillery is capable of producing two malts from stills similar to those at Littlemill.

PERSONAL NOTES

PRODUCT of SCOTLAND

Tullibardine

SINGLE HIGHLAND MALT SCOTCH WHISKY

A Single Malt Scotch Whisky of quality and distinction distilled and bottled by
TULLIBARDINE DISTILLERY LIMITED
BLACKFORD   PERTHSHIRE   SCOTLAND

40% VOL   750 ML

Brand	**TULLIBARDINE** (*Tully-bardeen*)
Distillery	Tullibardine BLACKFORD, Perthshire
Status	The Invergordon Distillers Ltd
Reception centre	No
Established	1949
Age when bottled	10 years
Strength	40%

TASTING NOTES

Nose	Delicate, mellow, sweet aroma of fruit.
Taste	Full-bodied, with a fruity flavour and a good lingering taste.
Comments	A pre-dinner dram from another distillery designed by W Delmé-Evans.

PERSONAL NOTES

THE WESTERN HIGHLANDS

Malt	**BEN NEVIS**
Distillery	Ben Nevis FORT WILLIAM, Inverness-shire
Status	Nikka Distillers, Japan
Reception centre	No
Established	c1825

TASTING NOTES (24 year old, 46%)

Nose	Full aroma of ripe fruit and sweetness.
Taste	Big, round and smooth with a dominating sweetness which suddenly fades away.
Comments	Rather a tantalising experience of fruit and spirit, almost a liqueur.

PERSONAL NOTES

Malt	**GLENLOCHY**
Distillery	Glenlochy FORT WILLIAM, Inverness-shire
Status	United Distillers
Reception centre	No
Established	1898

TASTING NOTES (26 year old, 46%)

Nose	Light and aromatic.
Taste	Light, spicy flavour which tends to finish quickly.
Comments	Pre-dinner drinking, but only from the independent bottlers (see page 139). The distillery is delightfully situated on the edge of the town.

PERSONAL NOTES

43% vol   75 cl ℮

Brand	**OBAN**
Distillery	Oban OBAN, Argyll
Status	United Distillers
Reception Centre	Yes. Tel: 0631–62110
Established	c1794
Age when bottled	14 years
Strength	43%

TASTING NOTES

Nose	Fresh hint of peat
Taste	Firm, malty flavour finishing very smoothly. Quite silky.
Comments	One of UD's Classic Malt range. An excellent anytime dram from a distillery founded by the Stevensons.

PERSONAL NOTES

THE LOWLANDS

The modern difference between Lowland malt and that originating from the other regions is simply one of style. Historically, the distinguishing factors were more numerous. In the late 18th century the product of the discreet Highland still (be it legal or illegal) was considered a wholesome, hand-crafted product which was in great demand in the urban markets, but the larger Lowland distillers produced a relatively coarse whisky (rarely made purely from malted barley alone) in huge industrial stills in an effort to supply both the city drinkers and the lucrative London market. This distinction was created by the industrial Lowland distillers who aggressively exploited whatever Government legislation was in force. The distinctions were magnified by the drawing of the "Highland Line" which effectively stretched from Greenock on the Clyde to Dundee on the Tay and split the country into two regions gauged by two separate sets of Excise regulations due to the disparity between their respective products.

Eventually the technical differences were removed when more realistic early-19th century Government Acts encouraged illicit distillers in the Highlands to go legal and allowed all producers to distil on a more equal basis. The massive grain distilleries of the central belt may be fewer now but they are still the sole remaining throwback to the days when the Steins and the Haigs wielded some of the most powerful industrial might in Scotland.

Although there is now a relatively low amount of distilling in the Lowlands, small malt distilleries were once in abundance even in the late 19th century. In the remote south west corner, over a dozen concerns existed stretching from Stranraer to Annan. Only Bladnoch Distillery survives and although the substantial remains of two distilleries at Langholm and Annan can still be viewed the

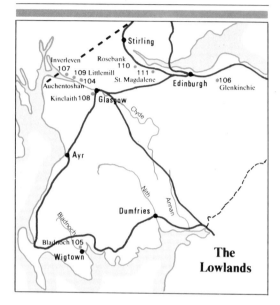

Distillery location numbers refer to page numbers.

malt they once produced has long been drunk away.

Fortunately we can still sample many good malts in the Lowland region. Scotland's most southerly is produced at Bladnoch, a beautifully located distillery with a new reception centre which is well worth the drive from Dumfries along the famous Solway coast. Just up the road from Bladnoch, at Girvan on the Ayrshire coast the less famous Ladyburn malt is produced beside Wm Grant's grain whisky distillery. Although bottled for export it can be obtained from the independent bottlers as well.

But most of the Lowland malts are produced to the north along the Highland line. In the Glasgow area, a visit to one of the malt distilleries near the city should not be missed. Just north of the Clyde along the A82 route to Loch Lomond lies Auchentoshan Distillery, which is one of the two Lowland distilleries still employing the technique of triple-distillation. This distillery caters well for the visitor with one of the first reception centres to be established in Scotland. Littlemill Distillery lies nearby, and employed triple distillation until the 1930's. Kinclaith malt still exists although the distillery is now no longer in existence having once been part of Long John's Strathclyde grain distilling complex. Another malt in a similar position is Inverleven which emanates from the curious Lomond stills at the malt distillery within Hiram Walker's vast grain distillery at Dumbarton. Rosebank, which lies nearer Edinburgh at Falkirk, is similar to Auchentoshan in that it too employs triple distillation and the result is one of the great Lowland malts, highly regarded as a pre-dinner dram and a wonderful surprise to anyone drinking their first malt whisky. Not far away at Linlithgow, St Magdalene has sadly been converted into accommodation, so this malt really will be a rarity.

Much of Edinburgh's prosperity has been built on brewing and distilling although the industry is greatly reduced within the city now. There are no malt distilleries operating now and all activity is concentrated in producing grain whisky. However, to the east of the city Glenkinchie Distillery at Pencaitland was one of the first to cater for visitors. It also has an interesting collection of museum pieces and gives a thorough insight into the "tools of the trade". This malt is bottled as a brand under the Classic Malt banner by UD, but all of them are worth looking out for and give a good indication of the Lowland style — light, fragant and an excellent way to start drinking malt whisky.

YRS **10** OLD

PRODUCT OF   SCOTLAND

AUCHENTOSHAN®
TRIPLE DISTILLED
SINGLE
LOWLAND MALT
SCOTCH WHISKY
DISTILLED & BOTTLED IN SCOTLAND
Auchentoshan Distillery
DALMUIR SCOTLAND

75 cl e   40% Vol

Brand	## AUCHENTOSHAN
Distillery	Auchentoshan DUNTOCHER, Dunbartonshire
Status	Morrison Bowmore Distillers Ltd
Reception Centre	Temporarily closed
Established	c1800
Age when bottled	10 & 21 years
Strength	10 year old — 40% 21 year old – 43%

TASTING NOTES (10 year old)

Nose	Delicate, slightly sweet.
Taste	Light, soft sweetness with a good aftertaste.
Comments	A triple-distilled malt from one of Scotland's most visited distilleries. Popular and readily available at home and abroad. If you're in Glasgow, drop in for a dram.

PERSONAL NOTES

Brand	**BLADNOCH**
Distillery	Bladnoch BLADNOCH, Wigtownshire
Status	United Distillers
Reception Centre	Yes. A charming place to visit. Tel: 09884–2235
Established	1817
Age when bottled	8 years
Strength	40%

TASTING NOTES

Nose	Very light and delicate.
Taste	Smooth, delicate but full and easy to drink.
Comments	Scotland's most southerly distillery. A pre-dinner malt which is now highly regarded — particularly the rare vintages.

PERSONAL NOTES

Brand	**GLENKINCHIE**
Distillery	Glenkinchie PENTCAITLAND East Lothian
Status	United Distillers
Reception Centre	Yes, and a museum. Tel: 0875–340333
Established	c1837
Age when bottled	10 years
Strength	43%

TASTING NOTES

Nose	Light fragrant sweetness.
Taste	Round flavour, slightly dry with a lingering smoothness.
Comments	An excellent pre-dinner dram, now available as a part of UD's Classic Malt range.

PERSONAL NOTES

Malt	**INVERLEVEN**
Distillery	Inverleven DUMBARTON, Strathclyde
Status	Allied Distillers Ltd
Reception Centre	No
Established	1938

TASTING NOTES (17 year old, 46%)

Nose	Delicate hint of smoke.
Taste	Quite full-bodied. Smooth with a round palate.
Comments	Rarely available unless obtained from the independent bottlers (see page 139).

PERSONAL NOTES

Glenkinchie Distillery

Brand	# KINCLAITH
Distillery	Kinclaith (dismantled 1975)
Status	1957–8

TASTING NOTES (18 year old, 46%)

Nose	Light and smokey with a spirit sharpness.
Taste	Full-bodied, smooth with an attractive finish.
Comments	From the independent bottlers (see page 139).

PERSONAL NOTES

Brand	**LITTLEMILL**
Distillery	Littlemill BOWLING, Dunbartonshire
Status	Gibson International Ltd
Reception Centre	No
Established	1772
Age when bottled	5 and 8 years
Strength	40%

TASTING NOTES (8 year old)

Nose	Light and delicate.
Taste	Mellow-flavoured, light, slightly cloying yet pleasant and warming.
Comments	Pre-dinner, from a distillery full of interesting, novel features. Certainly one of the oldest in Scotland.

PERSONAL NOTES

LOWLAND
SINGLE MALT
SCOTCH WHISKY

Established on its present site at CAMELON in 1840

ROSEBANK

distillery stands on the banks of the FORTH and CLYDE CANAL. This was once a busy thoroughfare with boats and steamers continually passing by; it is still the source of water for cooling. This single MALT SCOTCH WHISKY is triple distilled which accounts for its light distinctive nose and well balanced flavour.

AGED 12 YEARS

43% vol 70cl

Brand	**ROSEBANK**
Distillery	Rosebank Camelon, FALKIRK Stirlingshire
Status	United Distillers
Reception Centre	No. Visiting by appointment. Tel: 0324–23325.
Established	c1840
Age when bottled	12 years
Strength	43%

TASTING NOTES

Nose	Light, yet delicate.
Taste	Well balanced, good flavour with entirely acceptable astringency.
Comments	A triple-distilled malt suitable for pre-dinner drinking.

PERSONAL NOTES

Malt	**ST MAGDALENE**
Distillery	St Magdalene LINLITHGOW, West Lothian
Status	No longer licensed
Established	c1798

TASTING NOTES (20 year old, 46%)

Nose	A round aroma with a touch of smoke.
Taste	Full-bodied, smooth with a ripe finish and much character.
Comments	After-dinner malt. Again only from the independent bottlers (see page 139). The distillery has been converted into exclusive flats and apartments.

PERSONAL NOTES

ISLAY

O f all Scotland's malts, the Islays are perhaps the most easily recognised. But even so, there are some surprises within this group which are traditionally held to be amongst the heaviest and most pungent available. Their most recognisable characteristics are due to production methods which were developed in concert with the available distilling ingredients in this remote locality. While the mainland markets were supplied by mainland distillers in the 18th and 19th centuries, the islanders supplied a local market from stills — both legal and illegal — which were operated from farmyards, bothies on the bleak moors above Port Ellen and remote caves along the precipitous coast of the Oa.

Islay, renowned as the most fertile island in the Hebrides, had three major assets in this development, a ready source of local barley — or bere as it was then known — inexhaustible amounts of peat and burns running brim-full of soft water. Coupled to this was the likelihood that the art of distilling was probably brought to Scotland via Islay by the Irish in the 15th century. It is impossible to visit Islay and not notice the peat. Along the roadside crossing the enormous Laggan Bog between Port Ellen and Bowmore the peat banks spread as far as the eye can see. This fuel was the only means by which the islanders could dry their grain which was an essential process not only for distilling but also for storage during the wet seasons. By kilning barley it could be kept longer and the dryer the grain was, the less likely it was to go mouldy.

As the grain dried in the fumes, the peat imparted to the barley a highly distinctive character which manifested itself when the spirit was finally distilled from it. These characteristics are still apparent in today's Islay malts and are best

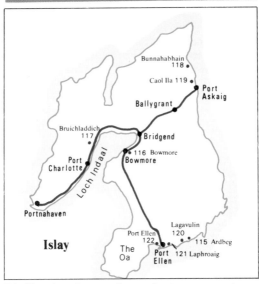

Bunnahabhain
118

Caol Ila 119

Port
Askaig

Ballygrant

Bruichladdich
117

Bridgend

Port
Charlotte

116 Bowmore
Bowmore

Loch Indaal

Portnahaven

Lagavulin
120

Port Ellen
122

115 Ardbeg

Islay

The
Oa

Port
Ellen

121 Laphroaig

Distillery location numbers refer to page numbers.

experienced by trying Ardbeg, Lagavulin and
Laphroaig which form the three most traditional
Islay malts. The other Islays display this peaty-
smokey characteristic to a lesser degree but it is
always detectable nonetheless.

It is good to see that the Islay distillers —
despite their more remote location — are always
able to accommodate visitors and some of the
distilleries are spectacularly situated. All of them
have one thing in common — they are built on the
seashore. A century ago this afforded them the
access to the sea and thus the mainland markets.
The smaller inland farmyard distilleries had by then
been unable to compete and one by one they closed
down. But it is still possible to see the sites of these
traditional distilleries, most notably at Octomore
Farm behind Port Charlotte, at Tallant Farm above
Bowmore and at Lossit Kennels by Bridgend. Of the

present distilleries perhaps Bowmore is most
favourably endowed for the visitor. Not only does it
produce a memorable dram but is has a superb
reception centre and has just constructed a
swimming pool in one of its old bonded warehouses
for the local community. In the south of the island
Lagavulin and Laphroaig both cater well for the
visitor and are magnificently located by the sea.
Ardbeg — about to produce again — is a more
sobering prospect given that the distillery was once
the centre of a large community. Port Ellen is still
closed but the associated maltings are at last being
put to better use and are supplying not only
Lagavulin and Caol Ila with malt, but also some of
the other non-UD distilleries on the island.

Across Loch Indaal from Bowmore lies
Bruichladdich which, like Bunnahabhain, produces
one of the lighter Islays. This distillery was one of
the first in the Hebrides to be constructed from
concrete in 1881. Near Port Askaig, at the point
where you cross to Jura, lie Caol Ila and
Bunnahabhain with spectacular views of the Paps
of Jura. Caol Ila is as modern and efficient a
distillery as you are likely to find and the stillhouse
alone is worth seeing. The dram is not readily
available but it is a good Islay as is its close
neighbour which was built in 1881. Bunnahabhain is
for many people the best introduction to the Islays
since it is neither too heavy nor too light, and for
many newcomers to the Islays it remains their
favourite dram.

A trip around Scotland's malts cannot be
considered complete unless the Islays are
undertaken with fervour for it is in their makeup
that the blender finds his greatest inspiration, the
enthusiast finds his greatest experience and the
taster finds his greatest joy.

Brand	**ARDBEG**
Distillery	Ardbeg PORT ELLEN, Islay, Argyll
Status	Allied Distillers Ltd
Reception Centre	No
Established	c1794
Age when bottled	10 years
Strength	40%

TASTING NOTES

Nose	Lovely peaty aroma with a hint of sweetness.
Taste	Full-bodied and luscious with an excellent aftertaste.
Comments	Good after-dinner malt. Perhaps the ultimate test for beginners?

PERSONAL NOTES

Brand	**BOWMORE**
Distillery	Bowmore BOWMORE, Islay, Argyll
Status	Morrison Bowmore Distillers Ltd
Reception Centre	Yes, the best in the islands. Tel: 049681–441
Established	c1770
Age when bottled	10, 12, 17 & 21 years
Strength	10 year old – 40% 12, 17 & 21 year old — 43%

TASTING NOTES

Nose	Light, peaty-smokey.
Taste	Healthy, middle-range Islay with medium weight and a smooth finish.
Comments	One of the best sherrying malts available — the older vintages are outstanding. The swimming pool in one of the bonds makes Bowmore a unique experience!

PERSONAL NOTES

PRODUCT OF SCOTLAND

BRUICHLADDICH

ISLAY

AGED 10 YEARS

SINGLE MALT
SCOTCH WHISKY

DISTILLED AND BOTTLED BY
BRUICHLADDICH DISTILLERY CO. LTD.
BRUICHLADDICH, ISLE OF ISLAY

Founded 1881

Brand	**BRUICHLADDICH** (*Broo-ick-laddie*)
Distillery	Bruichladdich BRUICHLADDICH, Islay, Argyll
Status	The Invergordon Distillers Ltd
Reception Centre	No, but visitors are always welcome. Tel: 049685–221
Established	1881
Age when bottled	10, 15 & 21 years old
Strength	40%

TASTING NOTES

Nose	Light to medium with a good hint of smoke.
Taste	Lingering flavour giving the expected fullness of Islay character whilst lacking the heavier tones.
Comments	A good pre-dinner dram, which is an ideal introduction to the Islay style.

PERSONAL NOTES

Brand	**BUNNAHABHAIN** (*Bu-na-ha-venn*)
Distillery	Bunnahabhain PORT ASKAIG, Islay, Argyll
Status	The Highland Distilleries Co plc
Reception Centre	Yes, but visitors by appointment. Tel: 049684–646
Established	c1881
Age when bottled	12 years
Strength	40%, 43% for export

TASTING NOTES

Nose	Pronounced character with a flowery aroma.
Taste	Not reminiscent of the Islay style, but a lovely round flavour nonetheless.
Comments	A popular after-dinner dram especially in France and the United States.

PERSONAL NOTES

ISLAY
SINGLE MALT SCOTCH WHISKY

CAOL ILA

distillery, built in 1846 is situated near *Port Askaig* on the *Isle of Islay*. Steamers used to call twice a week to collect *whisky* from this remote *site* in a cove facing the *Isle of Jura*. Water supplies for mashing come from *Loch nam Ban* although the sea provides water for *condensing*. Unusual for an *Islay* this *single MALT SCOTCH WHISKY* has a *fresh* aroma and a *light* yet well *rounded* flavour.

AGED **15** YEARS

43% vol Distilled & Bottled in SCOTLAND. CAOL ILA DISTILLERY Port Askaig, Isle of Islay, Scotland 70 cl

Brand	**CAOL ILA** (*Koal-eela*)
Distillery	Caol Ila PORT ASKAIG, Islay, Argyll
Status	United Distillers
Reception Centre	No. Visiting by appointment. Tel: 049684–207
Established	1864
Age when bottled	15 years
Strength	43%

TASTING NOTES (1969 distillation)

Nose	Light, fresh with a trace of peat.
Taste	Not a heavy Islay, but has pleasing weight and a fairly round flavour. Finishes smoothly.
Comments	Popular pre-dinner dram, readily available from the independent bottlers (see page 138) and at the distillery which is spectacularly situated on the Sound of Islay.

PERSONAL NOTES

Brand	**LAGAVULIN** (*Lagga-voolin*)
Distillery	Lagavulin PORT ELLEN, Islay, Argyll
Status	United Distillers
Reception centre	Yes. Visiting by appointment. Tel: 0496–2400.
Established	1816
Age when bottled	16 years
Strength	43%

TASTING NOTES

Nose	A typical Islay – heavy, powerful aroma. Unmistakable.
Taste	Quite heavy and very full with a delightful hint of sweetness at this age.
Comments	Part of UD's Classic Malt range. A gentle giant of a dram. One of the best.

PERSONAL NOTES

Brand	**LAPHROAIG** (*La-froyg*)
Distillery	Laphroaig PORT ELLEN, Islay, Argyll
Status	Allied Distillers Ltd
Reception centre	No, but visitors are always welcome. Tel: 0496–2418.
Established	1826
Age when bottled	10 and 15 years
Strength	40%, up to 45.1% for export.

TASTING NOTES (10 year old)

Nose	Well balanced, peaty-smokey.
Taste	Full of character, big Islay peaty flavour with a delightful touch of sweetness. Betrays its proximity to the sea.
Comments	An excellent after dinner malt from a beautifully situated distillery. Very popular.

PERSONAL NOTES

Malt	**PORT ELLEN**
Distillery	Port Ellen PORT ELLEN, Islay, Argyll
Status	United Distillers
Reception centre	No
Established	1825

TASTING NOTES (1969 distillation)

Nose	A hint of peat with a delicate bouquet
Taste	Light for an Islay lacking that characteristic peaty flavour. A dry finish.
Comments	A popular pre-dinner dram from the independent bottlers (see page 139). Direct exports to the Americas were first pioneered at Port Ellen in the 1840s. Distillery is still sadly closed.

PERSONAL NOTES

CAMPBELTOWN

Dufftown could lay claim to being Scotland's whisky capital but in the middle of the last century there was only one place which had the right to that name — Campbeltown.

Situated on the lee shore of the Mull of Kintyre, this town was literally awash with distillate a hundred years ago. When Alfred Barnard compiled his wonderful book — *The Whisky Distilleries of the United Kingdom* in 1886, he found no less than 21 producing distilleries in and around the town!

The number of operations were a throwback to the days when illicit distillation in the district was rife, and was not entirely discouraged by the landowners. Campbeltown's boom period was based upon a ready and huge market in cheap Scotch within the working population in the industrial central belt and the avaricious desire of the distillers to supply that market come what may. A local coal seam seemed perfect as a cheap source of fuel, but its exhaustion was to prove fatal, and as the late Victorian boom in whisky distilling collapsed so too did distilling in Campbeltown. The sad reminder of the industry's presence in the town is now manifested in two distilleries, Glen Scotia and Springbank, of which only the latter is still producing at the moment.

It would be unwise to forget Campbeltown's contribution to distilling despite the fact that it is unlikely more distilleries will ever start up in the town again. Its product had a unique regional flavour which came close to the Islay style. This can still be found in Longrow, a traditional old-fashioned malt which is distilled at Springbank. Its character differs from its sister malt Springbank which is a smoother, more elegant dram — one which has become phenomenally successful in Japan. That it has succeeded so well is a tribute to the family which has always owned the distillery

and which has always recognised its quality.

The drawings which appear here show something of the nature of distilling operations in the 'good old days' in the 1880's. When Barnard visited the town he noted that '' .... Sunday in Campbeltown is carried on to its Jewish length, and is quite a day of gloom and penance . . . it is said that there are as many places of worship as distilleries in the town''. His remarks, no matter how flippant, are important since they set down a precise record of the "Golden Age" of distilling in Scotland — a time we are unlikely to experience again. If Campbeltown's decline has served any purpose at all, it will have been to remind us all of the fickle nature of the marketplace.

As a town, Campbeltown is delightfully situated. Its remoteness allows its inhabitants a certain privacy from the mainstream tourist traffic during the summer, but it is always worth considering the detour down the Mull of Kintyre when travelling through this part of the world. The overwhelming impression is that of a thriving fishing and market town, but the names of old distilleries are to be found in a number of nameplaces — Ardlussa, Lochruan, Dalintober and

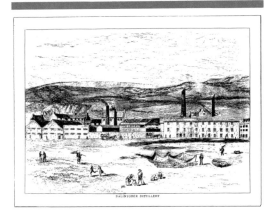

DALINTOBER DISTILLERY

the like. Savour them as you savour a dram in this setting — I have always said that drinking malt at source is the best way to appreciate it. Try it in Campbeltown.

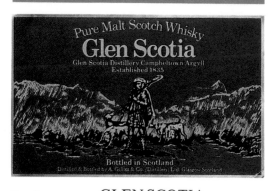

Brand	**GLEN SCOTIA**
Distillery	Glen Scotia CAMPBELTOWN, Argyll
Status	Gibson International Ltd
Reception centre	No
Established	c1832
Age when bottled	8 years
Strength	40%

TASTING NOTES

Nose	Faint touch of smoke. Intense aroma, but still delicate and sweet.
Taste	Light for a Campbeltown. Hint of peat with a good finish.
Comments	Pre-dinner dram. In fact, a good drink at any time.

PERSONAL NOTES

Brand	**LONGROW**
Distillery	Springbank CAMPBELTOWN, Argyll
Status	J & A Mitchell & Co Ltd
Reception centre	No
Established	c1824
Age when bottled	16 years
Strength	46%

TASTING NOTES

Nose	An island-peaty, medicinal aroma.
Taste	Well balanced, with a hint of sweetness. A succulent malty palate and a fine lingering aftertaste. Almost an Islay.
Comments	Distilled at Springbank, but by using entirely peat-dried malted barley, the heavier peated malt results. A dram for the connoisseur.

PERSONAL NOTES

Brand	# SPRINGBANK
Distillery	Springbank CAMPBELTOWN, Argyll
Status	J & A Mitchell & Co Ltd
Reception centre	No
Established	c1830
Age when bottled	15, 21, 25 & 30 years Export: 15, 21 & 33 years.
Strength	15, 21 & 30 years old — 46%; Export: 15 & 21 years old — 43%; 33 year old — 46%.

TASTING NOTES (21 year old, 46%)

Nose	Positive, rich aroma with a slight sweetness.
Taste	Well balanced, full of charm and elegance. A malt drinker's dream.
Comments	A dependable classic for the malt lover. Superb after-dinner drink — you won't refuse the second one! Bottled at the distillery and now widely available.

PERSONAL NOTES

THE ISLANDS AND N. IRELAND

Recent archaeological finds on the island of Rhum in the Inner Hebrides suggest that the natives knew how to make a brew long before the Irish were credited with introducing the art of distillation to their Scottish cousins. Wm Grant & Son Ltd (makers of Balvenie and Glenfiddich) even went so far as to try and recreate the original 4000 year old recipe which was scientifically reconstructed from scapings off pottery shards. The brew was drawn from the local herbs, grasses and other vegetation and turned out to be a little immature, but like all good brews it improved with familiarity. The last two centuries may have gradually familiarised the world to Scotch, but we can now lay claim to having played a fundamental part in the history of the development of distillation. And for the present-day visitor to Scotland, the past is manifested in some of the most gloriously situated distilleries in the world.

The styles of these malts differ, partly due to location and partly due to the desires of the distillery operators. For instance Jura, from the island just north of Islay, can be fairly described as a Highland-like dram whereas in the last century it was much closer in style to its Islay neighbours. The reason is that the distillery went out of production in 1901 and was replaced in 1963 with a completely new unit designed by W. Delmé-Evans. He had stills of a highland-type design installed and used malt that was only lightly peated. Similarly Tobermory's distillery has had its plant changed over the years and has produced some variable distillations of Ledaig until ceasing production in 1980. Happily, it is now back on stream.

On Skye an altogether more traditional taste is found. Talisker is one of the giants among malt. It is a 'big' whisky in every way with an explosive effect on the palate and a wonderful, peaty, sweetness on the nose. The distillery has changed considerably

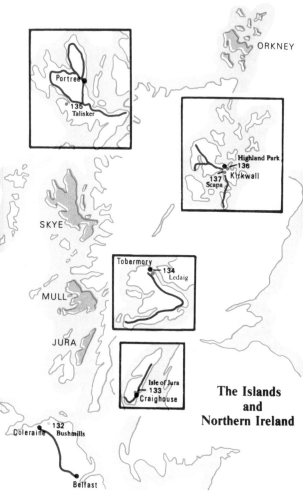

ORKNEY

Portree

135
Talisker

Highland Park
136
Kirkwall
137
Scapa

SKYE

Tobermory
134
Ledaig

MULL

JURA

Isle of Jura
133
Craighouse

The Islands
and
Northern Ireland

132
Coleraine Bushmills

Belfast

Distillery location numbers refer to page numbers.

but still retains some of the more traditional implements associated with 18th and 19th century distilling. For instance, swan-necked lyne arms can be seen dropping into wooden worm tubs outside the stillhouse wall — the same technique illicit distillers used though on a much smaller scale. Talisker's taste is perhaps the most recognisable among the island and western malts and has benefited greatly from the greater exposure it has undoubtedly received from its new-look packaging and presentation.

Orkney is the most northerly outpost of whisky distilling in Scotland with two very good malts emanating from Highland Park and Scapa. The surrounding Orcadian landscape at first sight appears bleak but its loveliness grows on the visitor just as their malts do. Their style is traditional — they are both very silky in texture and have a very faithful following among enthusiasts.

At the other geographical extreme across the North Channel from Galloway and only 17 miles (27Km) from Islay's southern shore lies another island — Ireland. Here, in County Antrim the oldest whiskey distillery in the world is producing a malt whiskey at Bushmills. It would be a nonsense to say it does not have a place in this book given that Islay (and therefore Scotland) probably owes much of its distilling heritage to Ireland. This dram is a pleasant surprise and should not be missed out. Within it I can detect subtle inferences from Islay, Campbeltown and Galloway and as such it should be accepted as part of the family. Notwithstanding that, the island malts show a tremendous variance in style and texture and are a good way to start an education of what is available to the malt drinker. To anyone who thinks that all malt whisky tastes the same, the island drams are a perfect answer.

Brand	**BUSHMILLS**
Distillery	Bushmills BUSHMILLS, Co Antrim N. Ireland
Status	Irish Distillers Ltd
Reception centre	Yes. Very popular. Advisable to telephone in advance. Tel: 02657–31521.
Established	1608
Age when bottled	10 years
Strength	40%

TASTING NOTES

Nose	Light, smokey, fragrant aroma.
Taste	Reflects the aroma. A very attractive lingering aftertaste of a well matured malt.
Comments	The only Irish malt whiskey from the oldest whiskey distillery in the world.

PERSONAL NOTES

Brand	**ISLE OF JURA**
Distillery	Isle of Jura Craighouse, JURA, Argyll
Status	The Invergordon Distillers Ltd
Reception centre	No, but visitors are welcome. Tel: 049682–240
Established	c1810, rebuilt in 1960–3
Age when bottled	10 years
Strength	40%

TASTING NOTES

Nose	Smooth with subtle peaty traces. Dry.
Taste	Well matured, full but delicate flavour. Good lingering character.
Comments	An almost Highland-like malt created by W Delmé-Evans for drinking anytime. Always worth visiting the distillery by crossing from Port Askaig when you are on Islay.

PERSONAL NOTES

Malt	**LEDAIG**
Distillery	Tobermory TOBERMORY, Mull, Argyll
Status	Tobermory Distillers Ltd
Reception centre	No
Established	1798

TASTING NOTES (No age given, 40%)

Nose	Fine, fruity nose.
Taste	Gentle flavour with a soft finish. A good, subtle malt.
Comments	Pre-dinner, from a distillery with a fascinating history. Available from the independent bottlers (see page 139). The distillery has been producing again since May 1990.

PERSONAL NOTES

Tobermory distillery, Isle of Mull

Brand	**TALISKER**
Distillery	Talisker CARBOST, Isle of Skye
Status	United Distillers
Reception centre	Yes. Tel: 047842–203
Established	1830–33
Age when bottled	10 years
Strength	45.8%

TASTING NOTES

Nose	Heavy sweet and full aroma.
Taste	Unique full flavour which explodes on the palate, lingering with an element of sweetness.
Comments	Superb after-dinner malt from UD's Classic Malt range. One of the best.

PERSONAL NOTES

Brand	**HIGHLAND PARK**
Distillery	Highland Park KIRKWALL, Orkney
Status	The Highland Distilleries Co plc
Reception centre	Yes. Tel: 0856–4619
Established	1795
Age when bottled	12 years
Strength	40%

TASTING NOTES

Nose	Full of character — pleasant, lingering and smokey.
Taste	Medium, well-balanced flavour finishing with a subtle dryness.
Comments	An excellent after-dinner dram from Scotland's most northerly distillery, now repackaged in a new bottle.

PERSONAL NOTES

Malt	**SCAPA**
Distillery	Scapa KIRKWALL, Orkney
Status	Allied Distillers Ltd
Reception centre	Tel: 0856–2071
Established	1885

TASTING NOTES (8 year old, 40%)

Nose	Delightful aromatic bouquet of peat and heather.
Taste	Medium-bodied with a malty, silk-like finish.
Comments	After-dinner, but only from the independent bottlers (see page 139). The Navy rescued Scapa from destruction by fire during the First World War!

PERSONAL NOTES

INDEPENDENT BOTTLERS

The following malts are not marketed as
commercial brands by their respective distillers and
are available from the two main Scottish
independent bottlers:

Gordon & MacPhail Ltd

50-60 South Street
ELGIN, Morayshire IV30 1JY
Tel: 0343-545111
Gordon and MacPhail usually give the year of
distillation instead of the age when bottled.
Strength is normally 40% alcohol by volume.

Cadenheads Whisky Shop

172 Canongate
EDINBURGH EH8 8BN
Tel: 031-556-5864 (retail & mixed cases)
Tel: 0586-52009 (wholesale)
William Cadenhead bottle malts at 46% alcohol by
volume, cask strength and at a number of ages.

	G & M	Wm Cad
Aberfeldy	1974	
Ardmore		22 years old
Balmenach	1970/71	
Banff	1974	14 years old
Ben Nevis		20, 24 years old
Benriach		21 years old
Benrinnes	1960/69	12, 23 years old
Benromach	1970	
Caol Ila	1974/75	12 years old
Caperdonich	1968/79	
Coleburn		17 years old
Convalmore	1969	
Craigellachie	1974	
Dailuaine		23 years old
Dallas Dhu	1973	

	G&M	Wm Cad
Glen Albyn	1968	23 years old
Glencadam	1974	23 years old
Glen Keith	1965	17, 22 years old
Glenlochy	1974	
Glenlossie	1971	
Glen Mhor	8, 15 years old	
Glentauchers		20 years old
Glenugie	1966	
Imperial	1970	
Inverleven		21 years old
Kinclaith	1967	
Ledaig	1972/73	
Lochside	1966	
Macduff	1975	
Millburn	1971	
Mortlach	15 years old 1960/1936	
Mosstowie	1970/75	
North Port	1970	
Old Pulteney	8 years old 1961	
Pittyvaich		13 years old
Port Ellen	1971	
Pulteney		17 years old
Royal Brackla	1970	
Scapa	8 years old	24 years old
Speyburn	1971	
St Magdalene	1965	
Teaninich	1975	

THE KEEPERS OF THE QUAICH

The Keepers of the Quaich is an exclusive society set up by the leaders of the Scotch whisky industry to honour those around the world who have contributed greatly to the standing and success of Scotch whisky.

It also aims to build on the value and prestige of Scotch whisky internationally and to further interest in the lesser known aspects and attitudes of the 'Spirits of Scotland'.

The organisation has members from 32 countries and includes leaders of the Scotch whisky industry and noted Scotch whisky connoisseurs and characters. All have one fundamental link in common — a love of Scotland and Scotch whisky. Under the patronage of (among others) His Grace, The Duke of Atholl, banquets are regularly held at Blair Castle in Perthshire to invest new members as Keepers and to promote not only Scotch but also Scotland. The seal of the society is therefore most appropriate — bestowed by the Lord Lyon, it proclaims UISGEBEATHA GU BRATH — Water of Life Forever.

FOUNDING PARTNERS

United Distillers
33 Ellersly Road
EDINBURGH EH12 6JW

United Distillers, the spirits company of Guinness plc, is the major producer of branded spirits in the UK with a portfolio of over 100 brands of Scotch whisky, gin, vodka and bourbon. UK sales are the responsibility of Perth-based United Distillers UK.

Allied Distillers Ltd
2 Glasgow Road
DUMBARTON G82 1ND

Incorporating George Ballantine & Son, William
Teacher & Sons and Stewart & Son of Dundee this
new company formed in January 1988 focuses the
inter-related whisky interests of Hiram Walker-
Allied Vintners, the wines and spirits arm of Allied-
Lyons plc. Headquartered in Dumbarton where the
parent company operates the largest grain whisky
distillery in Scotland, the new company continues
an association with the town first started in 1938 by
Hiram Walker.

Justerini & Brooks Ltd
151 Marylebone Road
LONDON NW1 5QE

This company was founded in 1749 by Giacomo
Justerini, an Italian cordial maker who came to
London in pursuit of an Opera singer. He failed in
his quest for the lady, but remained to form a
commercial alliance with George Johnson and
together they set themselves up as wine merchants.
By 1760 the company had been granted the first of
its eight Royal Warrants and in 1830 the company
was bought by Alfred Brooks. A century later the
house brand of Scotch — J & B Rare dominated the
company's exports to the United States. After
merging with Twiss Brownings and Hallowes to
form United Wine Traders, the company bought
Gilbeys in 1962 to form International Distillers and
Vintners, now the drinks division of Grand
Metropolitan.

**The Highland Distilleries Co plc &
Robertson & Baxter Ltd
106 West Nile Street
GLASGOW G1 2QY**

The Highland Distilleries Company was
incorporated in July 1887 as distillers of high quality
malt whisky for the blending trade having secured
the ownership of both Glenrothes and
Bunnahabhain distilleries. Having acquired
Glenglassaugh distillery in 1892 and Tamdhu in
1898, the company expanded its interests and later
formed a close association with whisky brokers
Robertson & Baxter Ltd. The malt portfolio was
enlarged with the addition of Highland Park in
Orkney in 1937 and its blended whisky interests
were also furthered with the takeover of Matthew
Gloag & Son Ltd, the Perth blenders of the Famous
Grouse in 1970.

CORPORATE MEMBERS

**Berry Bros & Rudd Ltd
3 St James's Street
LONDON SW1A 1EG**

**Burn Stewart Distillers plc
65 Kelburn Street
GLASGOW G78 1LD**

**Campbell Distillers Ltd
West Byrehill
KILWINNING KA13 6LE**

**Findlater Mackie Todd & Co Ltd
Deerpark Road
Merton Abbey
LONDON SW19 3TU**

**J & G Grant
Glenfarclas Distillery
Marypark
BALLINDALLOCH
Banffshire AB3 9BD**

William Grant & Sons Ltd
Independence House
84 Lower Mortlake Road
RICHMOND TW9 2HS

Invergordon Distillers Ltd
9–12 Salamander Place
EDINBURGH EH6 7JL

Inver House Distillers Ltd
Towers Road
AIRDRIE ML6 8PL

William Lawson Distillers Ltd
288 Main Street
COATBRIDGE ML5 3RH

Macallan Glenlivet plc
CRAIGELLACHIE
Banffshire AB3 9RX

Macdonald Martin Distillers plc
186 Commercial Street
Leith
EDINBURGH EH6 6NN

Morrison Bowmore Distillers Ltd
Springburn Bond
Carlisle Street
GLASGOW G21 1EQ

The North British Distillery Co Ltd
Wheatfield Road
EDINBURGH EH11 2PX

The Chivas and Glenlivet Group
111 Renfrew Road
PAISLEY PA3 4DY

The Tomatin Distillery Co Ltd
TOMATIN
Invernesshire IV13 7YT

Whyte & Mackay Distillers Ltd
Dalmore House
296/298 St Vincent Street
GLASGOW G2 5RG

INDEX